A CHILD'S BOOK OF CAROLS

Accompaniments arranged by
HUBERT J. FOSS

KU-707-943

OXFORD UNIVERSITY PRESS
LONDON   NEW YORK   TORONTO

JAMES HAWORTH & BROTHER, LTD., LONDON

AND TO THE EARTH BE PEACE

CHAMELEON BOOKS

7

A CHILD'S
BOOK OF CAROLS

Many of the Carols printed in this book will be found in the " Oxford Book of Carols ", in a different arrangement.

To the Editors, Dr R. Vaughan Williams, O.M., Dr Martin Shaw, and the late Dr Percy Dearmer's executors, thanks are due for permission to reprint copyright material, and as well to certain translators, Mr Robert Graves and Mr Steuart Wilson especially.

CONTENTS

SUNNY BANK

As I sat on a sunny bank, As I sat on a sunny bank, As I sat on a sunny bank, On Christ - mas Day in the morn - ing.

2 I spied three ships come sailing by,
   On Christmas Day in the morning.

3 And who should be with those three ships
   But Joseph and his fair lady!

4 O he did whistle, and she did sing,
   On Christmas Day in the morning.

5 And all the bells on earth did ring,
   On Christmas Day in the morning.

6 For joy that our Saviour he was born
   On Christmas Day in the morning.

God rest you mer-ry gen-tle-men, Let no-thing you dis-may, Re-mem-ber Christ our Sa-viour Was born on Christ-mas Day, To save poor souls from Sa-tan's power Which had long gone a-stray, And it's ti-dings of com-fort and joy, comfort and joy, And it's ti-dings of com-fort and joy.

2 From God that is our Father,
     The blessèd Angels came,
Unto some certain Shepherds,
     With tidings of the same;
That there was born in Bethlehem,
     The Son of God by name.
And it's tidings of comfort and joy,

3 Go, fear not, said God's Angels,
     Let nothing you affright,
For there is born in Bethlehem,
     Of a pure Virgin bright,
One able to advance you,
     And threw down Satan quite.
And it's tidings of comfort and joy.

4 The Shepherds at those tidings,
     Rejoiced much in mind,
And left their flocks a-feeding
     In tempest storms of wind,
And straight they came to Bethlehem,
     The son of God to find.
And it's tidings of comfort and joy.

5 Now when they came to Bethlehem,
     Where our sweet Saviour lay,
They found him in a manger,
     Where Oxen feed on hay,
The blessed Virgin kneeling down,
     Unto the Lord did pray.
And it's tidings of comfort and joy.

6 With sudden joy and gladness,
     The Shepherds were beguil'd,
To see the Babe of Israel,
     Before his Mother mild,
On them with joy and cheerfulness,
     Rejoice each Mother's Child.
And it's tidings of comfort and joy.

7 Now to the Lord sing praises,
     All you within this place,
Like we true loving Brethren,
     Each other to embrace,
For the merry time of Christmas
     Is drawing on apace.
And it's tidings of comfort and joy.

8 God bless the ruler of this house,
     And send him long to reign,
And many a merry Christmas
     May live to see again.
Among your friends and kindred,
     That live both far and near,
And God send you a happy New Year.

THE FIRST NOWELL

The first Nowell the angel did say Was to certain poor shepherds in fields as they lay; In fields where they lay, keeping their sheep, In a cold winter's night that was so deep:

Refrain

Nowell, Nowell, Nowell, Nowell, Born is the King of Israel!

1　The first Nowell the angel did say
　　Was to certain poor shepherds in fields as they lay;
　　In fields where they lay, keeping their sheep,
　　In a cold winter's night that was so deep:
　　Nowell, Nowell, Nowell, Nowell,
　　Born is the King of Israel!

2　They looked up and saw a star,
　　Shining in the east, beyond them far;
　　And to the earth it gave great light,
　　And so it continued both day and night.

3　And by the light of that same star,
　　Three Wise Men came from country far;
　　To seek for a king was their intent,
　　And to follow the star wheresoever it went:

4　This star drew nigh to the north-west;
　　O'er Bethlehem it took its rest,
　　And there it did both stop and stay
　　Right over the place where Jesus lay:

5　Then did they know assuredly
　　Within that house the King did lie:
　　One entered in then for to see,
　　And found the babe in poverty:

6　Then entered in those Wise Men three,
　　Fell reverently upon their knee,
　　And offered there in his presence
　　Both gold and myrrh and frankincense:

7　Between an ox-stall and an ass
　　This child truly there born he was;
　　For want of clothing they did him lay
　　All in the manger, among the hay.

8　Then let us all with one accord
　　Sing praises to our heavenly Lord,
　　That hath made heaven and earth of naught,
　　And with his blood mankind hath bought:

WHILE SHEPHERDS WATCHED

1 While shepherds watched their flocks by night,
      All seated on the ground,
   The Angel of the Lord came down,
      And glory shone around.
   ' Fear not ', said he (for mighty dread
      Had seized their troubled mind);
   ' Glad tidings of great joy I bring
      To you and all mankind.

2 ' To you in David's town this day
      Is born of David's line
   A Saviour, who is Christ the Lord;
      And this shall be the sign:
   The heavenly Babe you there shall find
      To human view displayed,
   All meanly wrapped in swathing bands,
      And in a manger laid.'

3. Thus spake the Seraph: and forthwith
      Appeared a shining throng
   Of angels praising God, who thus
      Addressed their joyful song:
   ' All glory be to God on high,
      And to the earth be peace;
   Good-will henceforth from heaven to men
      Begin and never cease.'

NOS CALAN
Welsh Carol

Worlds ___ his might - y voice o - beyed;

Laws, which nev - er shall be bro - ken,

For ___ their guid - ance hath he made.

1 Praise the Lord! Ye heav'ns adore him;
   Praise him, angels in the height;
Sun and moon, rejoice before him;
   Praise him, all ye stars and light:
Praise the Lord, for he hath spoken;
   Worlds his mighty voice obeyed;
Laws, which never shall be broken,
   For their guidance hath he made.

2 Praise the Lord! for he is glorious;
   Never shall his promise fail;
God hath made his Saints victorious,
   Sin and death shall not prevail.
Praise the God of our salvation;
   Hosts on high, his power proclaim;
Heaven and earth, and all creation,
   Laud and magnify his name!

9

THE HOLLY AND THE IVY

The hol-ly and the I-vy, Now both are full-well grown,— Of all the trees that are in the wood, The hol-ly bears the crown:— O the ris-ing of the sun The run-ning of the deer, The play-ing of the merry organ, Sweet sing-ing in the choir, Sweet sing-ing in the choir.

1 The holly and the ivy,
  Now both are full well grown,
  Of all the trees that are in the wood,
  The holly bears the crown:

  O the rising of the sun
  The running of the deer,
  The playing of the merry organ,
  Sweet singing in the choir.

2 The holly bears a blossom,
  As white as the lily flower,
  And Mary bore sweet Jesus Christ,
  To be our sweet Saviour:

3 The holly bears a berry,
  As red as any blood,
  And Mary bore sweet Jesus Christ
  To do poor sinners good:

4 The holly bears a prickle,
  As sharp as any thorn,
  And Mary bore sweet Jesus Christ
  On Christmas day in the morn:

5 The holly bears a bark,
  As bitter as any gall,
  And Mary bore sweet Jesus Christ
  For to redeem us all:

6 The holly and the ivy,
  Now both are full well grown,
  Of all the trees that are in the wood,
  The holly bears the crown:

I SAW THREE SHIPS

I saw three ships come sail - ing in, On
Christ - mas Day, on Christ - mas Day, I
saw three ships come sail - ing in, On
Christ - mas Day in the morn - ing.

1 I saw three ships come sailing in,
   On Christmas Day, on Christmas Day,
   I saw three ships come sailing in,
   On Christmas Day in the morning.

2 And what was in those ships all three?

3 Our Saviour Christ and his lady.

4 Pray, whither sailed those ships all three?

5 O, they sailed into Bethlehem.

6 And all the bells on earth shall ring,

7 And all the angels in Heaven shall sing,

8 And all the souls on earth shall sing.

9 Then let us all rejoice amain!

SEVEN JOYS

The first good joy that Ma - ry had,

It was the joy of one;

To see the bless - ed Je - sus Christ

When he was first ___ her son. ___

When he was first her son, good man, And bless - ed may he

be, _____ Both Fa-ther, Son and

Ho- ly Ghost to all e-ter- ni- ty. _____

2   The next good joy that Mary had,
      It was the joy of two;
   To see her own son, Jesus Christ
     To make the lame to go:

3   The next good joy that Mary had,
      It was the joy of three;
   To see her own son, Jesus Christ
     To make the blind to see:

4   The next good joy that Mary had,
      It was the joy of four;
   To see her own son, Jesus Christ
     To read the Bible o'er:

5   The next good joy that Mary had,
      It was the joy of five;
   To see her own son, Jesus Christ
     To bring the dead alive:

6   The next good joy that Mary had,
      It was the joy of six;
   To see her own son, Jesus Christ
     Upon the Crucifix:

7   The next good joy that Mary had,
      It was the joy of seven;
   To see her own son, Jesus Christ
     To wear the crown of heaven:

WONDROUS WORKS

When Je - sus Christ was twelve years old, As ho - ly Scrip-ture plain - ly told, _____ He then dis - pu - ted brave and bold A - mongst the learn - ed doc - tors:

Refrain

Then praise the Lord both high and low, 'Cause he his won - drous works doth show, _____ That we at last to heaven might go, Where Christ in glo - ry reign - eth.

1   When Jesus Christ was twelve years old,
    As holy Scripture plainly told,
    He then disputed brave and bold
       Amongst the learnèd doctors:

Then praise the Lord both high and low,
*   'Cause he his wondrous works doth shew.*
That we at last to heaven might go,
*   Where Christ in glory reigneth.*

2   At thirty years he then began
    To preach the Gospel unto man,
    And all Judaea wondered then
       To hear his heavenly doctrine:

3   The woman's son, that dead did lie,
    When Christ our Saviour passèd by,
    He rose to life immediately,
       To her great joy and comfort:

4   Likewise he healed the lepers ten,
    Whose bodies were full filthy then;
    And there returnèd back but one
       Him humble thanks to render:

5   More of his heavenly might to shew,
    Himself upon the sea did go;
    And there was none that e'er did so,
       But only Christ our Saviour:

PATAPAN

Wil - lie, take your lit - tle drum, With your whis-tle Rob - in come! When we hear the fife and drum, Tu - re - lu - re - lu, pa - ta - pa - ta- -pan, When we hear the fife and drum, Christmas should be ___ fro - lic - some.

1 Willie, take your little drum,
  With your whistle, Robin, come!
      When we hear the fife and drum,
      Ture-lure-lu, pata-pata-pan,
          When we hear the fife and drum,
          Christmas should-be frolicsome.

2 Thus the men of olden days
  Loved the King of kings to praise:
      When they hear the fife and drum,
      Ture-lure-lu, pata-pata-pan,
          When they hear the fife and drum,
          Sure our children won't be dumb!

3 God and man are now become
  More at one than fife and drum.
      When you hear the fife and drum,
      Ture-lure-lu, Pata-pata-pan,
          When you hear the fife and drum,
          Dance, and make the village hum!

SONG OF THE SHIP

There comes a ship a-sail-ing With an-gels fly-ing fast; She bears a splen-did car-go And has a might-y mast.

1   There comes a ship a-sailing
     With angels flying fast;
She bears a splendid cargo
     And has a mighty mast.

2   This ship is fully laden,
     Right to her highest board;
She bears the Son from heaven,
     God's high eternal Word.

3   Upon the sea unruffled
     The ship moves in to shore,
To bring us all the riches
     She has within her store.

4   And that ship's name is Mary,
     Of flowers the rose is she,
And brings to us her baby
     From sin to set us free.

5   The ship made in this fashion,
     In which such store was cast,
Her sail is love's sweet passion,
     The Holy Ghost her mast.

GOOD KING WENCESLAS

Good King Wen-ces-las looked out, On the feast of Ste-phen,

When the snow lay round a-bout, Deep, and crisp, and ev-en:

Brightly shone the moon that night, Though the frost was cru-el,

When a poor man came in sight, Gathering winter fu-el.

1   Good King Wenceslas looked out,
    On the Feast of Stephen,
  When the snow lay round about,
    Deep, and crisp, and even:
  Brightly shone the moon that night,
    Though the frost was cruel,
  When a poor man came in sight,
    Gathering winter fuel.

2   ' Hither, page, and stand by me,
    If thou know'st it, telling,
  Yonder peasant, who is he?
    Where and what his dwelling? '
  ' Sire, he lives a good league hence,
    Underneath the mountain,
  Right against the forest fence,
    By Saint Agnes' fountain.'

3   ' Bring me flesh, and bring me wine,
    Bring me pine-logs hither:
  Thou and I will see him dine,
    When we bear them thither.'
  Page and monarch, forth they went,
    Forth they went together;
  Through the rude wind's wild lament
    And the bitter weather

4   ' Sire, the night is darker now,
    And the wind blows stronger;
  Fails my heart, I know not how;
    I can go no longer.'
  ' Mark my footsteps, good my page;
    Tread thou in them boldly:
  Thou shalt find the winter's rage
    Freeze thy blood less coldly.'

5   In his master's steps he trod,
    Where the snow lay dinted;
  Heat was in the very sod
    Which the Saint had printed.
  Therefore, Christian men, be sure,
    Wealth or rank possessing,
  Ye who now will bless the poor,
    Shall yourselves find blessing.

IN EXCELSIS GLORIA

A. H. BROWN

When Christ was born of Ma-ry free, In Beth-lem in that fair ci-ty, An-gels sung e'er with mirth and glee, *In ex-cel-sis glo-ri-a,*

Chorus

In ex-cel-sis glo-ri-a, In ex-cel-sis

glo - ri - a, In ex - cel - sis glo - ri - a,

In ex - cel - sis glo - ri - a. D.S.

Christo paremus cantica
In excelsis gloria.

1 When Christ was born of Mary free,
   In Bethlehem in that fair city,
   Angels sung e'er with mirth and glee,
      In excelsis gloria.

2 Herdmen beheld these angels bright—
   To them appearèd with great light,
   And said, ' God's son is born this night ':

3 This king is come to save his kind,
   In the scripture as we find ;
   Therefore this song have we in mind :

4 Then, dear Lord, for thy great grace,
   Grant us the bliss to see thy face,
   Where we may sing to thy solace :

MID-WINTER

In moderate time

GUSTAV HOLST

In the bleak mid - win - ter

Frost - y wind made moan, Earth stood hard as

ir - on, Wa - ter like a stone;

Snow had fal - len, snow on snow, Snow_ on_ snow,

In the bleak mid - win - ter, Long_ a - go.

1 In the bleak mid-winter
      Frosty wind made moan,
   Earth stood hard as iron,
      Water like a stone;
   Snow had fallen, snow on snow,
      Snow on snow,
   In the bleak mid-winter,
      Long ago.

2 Our God, heaven cannot hold him
      Nor earth sustain;
   Heaven and earth shall flee away
      When he comes to reign:
   In the bleak mid-winter
      A stable-place sufficed
   The Lord God Almighty
      Jesus Christ.

3 Enough for him, whom Cherubim
      Worship night and day,
   A breastful of milk,
      And a mangerful of hay;
   Enough for him, whom Angels
      Fall down before,
   The ox and ass and camel
      Which adore.

4 Angels and Archangels
      May have gathered there,
   Cherubim and Seraphim
      Thronged the air:
   But only his mother
      In her maiden bliss
   Worshipped the Belovèd
      With a kiss.

5 What can I give him,
      Poor as I am?
   If I were a shepherd
      I would bring a lamb,
   If I were a wise man
      I would do my part:
   Yet what I can I give him—
      Give my heart.

KINGS OF ORIENT

We three kings of O - ri - ent are, Bear - ing gifts we tra-verse a - far Field and foun - tain, moor and moun - tain, Fol - low-ing yon - der star:

Refrain (after each verse)

O_____ star of won - der, star of night, Star with roy - al beau - ty bright, West - ward lead - ing, still pro - ceed - ing, Guide us to thy per - fect light.

THE KINGS:

1   We three kings of Orient are;
Bearing gifts we traverse afar
Field and fountain, moor and mountain,
Following yonder star:

> *O star of wonder, star of night,*
> *Star with royal beauty bright,*
> *Westward leading, still proceeding,*
> *Guide us to thy perfect light.*

MELCHIOR:

2   Born a king on Bethlehem plain,
Gold I bring, to crown him again
King for ever, ceasing never,
Over us all to reign:

GASPAR:

3   Frankincense to offer have I;
Incense owns a Deity nigh:
Prayer and praising, all men raising,
Worship him, God most high:

BALTHAZAR:

4   Myrrh is mine; its bitter perfume
Breathes a life of gathering gloom;
Sorrowing, sighing, bleeding, dying,
Sealed in the stone-cold tomb:

ALL:

5   Glorious now, behold him arise,
King, and God, and sacrifice!
Heaven sings alleluya,
Alleluya the earth replies:

FURRY DAY CAROL

(Spring Carol)

Re - mem - ber__ us poor May - ers__ all! And__ thus we do__ be - gin - a To lead our__ lives in__ right-eous-ness, Or__ else we die__ in__ sin__ a: With Ho - lan - to, sing__ mer - ry,__ O, With__ Ho - lan - to,__ sing__ mer - ry, With Ho - lan - to, sing mer - ry,__ O, With Ho - lan - to, sing mer - ry!

1   Remember us poor Mayers all!
     And thus we do begin-a
  To lead our lives in righteousness,
     Or else we die in sin-a:

> *With Holan-to, sing merry, O,*
> *With Holan-to, sing merry,*
>   *With Holan-to, sing merry, O,*
> *With Holan-to, sing merry !*

2   We have been rambling half the night,
     And almost all the day-a,
  And now, returnèd back again,
     We've brought you a branch of May-a:

3   O, we were up as soon as day,
     To fetch the summer home-a;
  The summer is a-coming on,
     And winter is agone-a:

4   Then let us all most merry be,
     And sing with cheerful voice-a;
  For we have good occasion now
     This time for to rejoice-a:

5   Saint George he next shall be our song:
     Saint George, he was a knight-a;
  Of all the men in Christendom
     Saint George he was the right-a:

6   God bless our land with power and might,
     God send us peace in England;
  Pray send us peace both day and night,
     For ever in merry England:

GREENSLEEVES
(New Year)

The old year now away is fled, The new year it is en-ter-ed; Then let us now our sins down-tread, And joy-ful-ly all ap-pear: Let's mer-ry be this day, And let us now both sport and play: Hang grief, cast care a-way! God

send   you   a   hap - py New   Year! _____

1   The old year now away is fled,
      The new year it is enterèd;
   Then let us now our sins down-tread,
      And joyfully all appear:
        Let's merry be this day,
        And let us now both sport and play:
        Hang grief, cast care away!
          God send you a happy New Year!

2   The name-day now of Christ we keep,
      Who for our sins did often weep;
   His hands and feet were wounded deep,
      And his blessèd side with a spear;
        His head they crowned with thorn,
        And at him they did laugh and scorn,
        Who for our good was born:
          God send us a happy New Year!

3   And now with New Year's gifts each friend
      Unto each other they do send:
   God grant we may all our lives amend,
      And that the truth may appear.
        Now, like the snake, your skin
        Cast off, of evil thoughts and sin,
        And so the year begin:
          God send us a happy New Year!

THE BELLMAN'S SONG

The moon shines bright, and the stars give a light: A
lit-tle be - fore it was day Our
Lord, our God, he called on us, And
bid us a - wake and pray.

1   The moon shines bright, and the stars give a light:
        A little before it was day
    Our Lord, our God, he called on us,
        And bid us awake and pray.

2   Awake, awake, good people all;
        Awake, and you shall hear,
    Our Lord, our God, died on the cross
        For us whom he loved so dear.

3   O fair, O fair Jerusalem,
        When shall I come to thee?
    When shall my sorrows have an end,
        Thy joy that I may see?

4   The fields were green as green could be,
        When from his glorious seat
    Our Lord, our God, he watered us,
        With his heavenly dew so sweet.

5   And for the saving of our souls
        Christ died upon the cross;
    We ne'er shall do for Jesus Christ
        As he hath done for us.

6   The life of man is but a span
        And cut down in its flower;
    We are here to-day, and tomorrow are gone,
        The creatures of an hour.

O LITTLE TOWN

O lit - tle town of Beth - le - hem,
A - bove thy deep and dream - less sleep

How still we see thee lie!
The si - lent stars go by.

Yet in thy dark streets shin - eth

The ev - er - last - ing light; The hopes and fears of

all the years Are met in thee to - night.

1 O little town of Bethlehem,
  How still we see thee lie!
 Above thy deep and dreamless sleep
  The silent stars go by.
 Yet in thy dark streets shineth
  The everlasting light;
 The hopes and fears of all the years
  Are met in thee to-night.

2 O morning stars, together
  Proclaim the holy birth,
 And praises sing to God the King,
  And peace to men on earth;
 For Christ is born of Mary;
  And, gathered all above,
 While mortals sleep, the angels keep
  Their watch of wondering love.

3 How silently, how silently,
  The wondrous gift is given!
 So God imparts to human hearts
  The blessings of his heaven.
 No ear may hear his coming;
  But in this world of sin,
 Where meek souls will receive him, still
  The dear Christ enters in.

4 Where children pure and happy
  Pray to the blessèd Child,
 Where misery cries out to thee,
  Son of the mother mild;
 Where charity stands watching
  And faith holds wide the door,
 The dark night wakes, the glory breaks,
  And Christmas comes once more.

5 O holy Child of Bethlehem,
  Descend to us, we pray;
 Cast out our sin, and enter in,
  Be born in us to-day.
 We hear the Christmas Angels
  The great glad tidings tell:
 O come to us, abide with us,
  Our Lord Emmanuel.

20 HE IS BORN, THE CHILD DIVINE

Il est né le Divin Enfant

He is born, the child Di - vine,

Sing out o - boe, sound bas-soon, He is born, the

child di - vine, Voi - ces prais-ing him en - twine.

Since be - yond four thou-sand years Pro-phets have pro -

-claimed his com - ing; Since be - yond four

38

thou-sand years Wait-ed have our cag-er ears.

D.C. al Fine

1 He is born, the child Divine,
    Sing out oboe, sound bassoon;
    He is born, the child Divine,
    Voices praising him entwine.

2 Since beyond four thousand years
    Prophets have proclaimed his coming;
    Since beyond four thousand years
    Waited have our eager ears.

        He is born, the Child Divine,
        Sing out oboe, sound bassoon;
        He is born, the child Divine,
        Voices praising him entwine.

3 He was lodged in stable base,
    Just a little straw his bed;
    He was lodged in stable base,
    Humble is God's resting place.

4 Beautiful this infant is,
    Perfect in his manliness;
    Beautiful this infant is,
    Virtue touches all that's his.

THE PRAISE OF CHRISTMAS

All hail to the days that mer - it more praise Than all the rest of the year,___ And wel - come the nights that dou - ble de-lights As well for the poor as the peer!___ Good for - tune at - tend each mer - ry man's friend That doth but the best that he may, For - get - ting old wrongs with

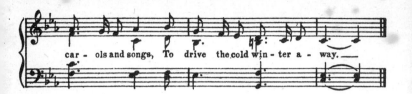

car - ols and songs, To drive the cold win - ter a - way.

1. All hail to the days that merit more praise
   Than all the rest of the year,
   And welcome the nights that double delights
   As well for the poor as the peer!
   Good fortune attend each merry man's friend
   That doth but the best that he may,
   Forgetting old wrongs with carols and songs,
   To drive the cold winter away.

2. 'Tis ill for a mind to anger inclined
   To think of small injuries now;
   If wrath be to seek, do not lend her thy cheek,
   Nor let her inhabit thy brow.
   Cross out of thy books malevolent looks,
   Both beauty and youth's decay,
   And wholly consort with mirth and with sport,
   To drive the cold winter away.

3. This time of the year is spent in good cheer,
   And neighbours together do meet,
   To sit by the fire, with friendly desire,
   Each other in love to greet.
   Old grudges forgot are put in the pot,
   All sorrows aside they lay;
   The old and the young doth carol this song,
   To drive the cold winter away.

4. When Christmas's tide comes in like a bride,
   With holly and ivy clad,
   Twelve days in the year much mirth and good cheer
   In every household is had.
   The country guise is then to devise
   Some gambols of Christmas play,
   Whereat the young men do best that they can
   To drive the cold winter away.

22

SONG OF THE CRIB

Jo - seph dear - est, Jo - seph mine, Help me cra - dle the child di - vine; God re - ward thee and all that's thine In Par - a - dise, So prays the mo - ther Ma - ry.

He came a - mong us at Christ - mas tide, At Christ - mas tide, In Beth - le - hem; Men shall bring him from far and wide Love's di - a - dem: Je - sus, Je - sus, Lo, he comes, and loves, and saves, and frees us.

2 Gladly, dear one, lady mine,
Help I cradle this child of thine;
God's own light on us both shall shine
   In Paradise,
      As prays the mother Mary.

CHORUS
He came among us at Christmas tide,
   At Christmas tide,
      In Bethlehem;
Men shall bring him from far and wide
     Love's diadem:
    Jesus, Jesus,
Lo, he comes, and loves, and saves, and frees us!

3 SERVANT (1)
Peace to all that have goodwill!
God, who heaven and earth doth fill,
Comes to turn us away from ill,
   And lies so still
      Within the crib of Mary.

4 SERVANT (2)
All shall come and bow the knee;
Wise and happy their souls shall be,
Loving such a divinity,
   As all may see
      In Jesus, Son of Mary.

5 SERVANT (3)
Now is born Emmanuel,
Prophesied once by Ezekiel,
Promised Mary by Gabriel—
   Ah, who can tell
      Thy praises, Son of Mary!

6 SERVANT (4)
Thou my lazy heart hast stirred,
Thou, the Father's eternal Word,
Greater than aught that ear hath heard,
   Thou tiny bird
      Of love, thou Son of Mary.

7 SERVANT (1)
Sweet and lovely little one,
Thou princely, beautiful, God's own Son,
Without thee all of us were undone;
   Our love is won
      By thine, O Son of Mary.

8 SERVANT (2)
Little man, and God indeed,
Little and poor, thou art all we need;
We will follow where thou dost lead,
   And we will heed
      Our brother, born of Mary.

23

THE CRADLE

He smiles with-in his cra - dle, A babe with face so bright It beams most like a mir - ror A - gainst a blaze of light: This babe so burn - ing bright.

1   He smiles within his cradle,
     A babe with face so bright
     It beams most like a mirror
     Against a blaze of light:
     This babe so burning bright.

2   This babe we now declare to you
     Is Jesus Christ our Lord;
     He brings both peace and heartiness:
     Haste, haste with one accord
     To feast with Christ our Lord.

3   And who would rock the cradle
     Wherein this infant lies,
     Must rock with easy motion
     And watch with humble eyes,
     Like Mary pure and wise.

4.   O Jesus, dearest babe of all
     And dearest babe of mine,
     Thy love is great, thy limbs are small.
     O, flood this heart of mine
     With overflow from thine!

24

CAROL OF SERVICE

Up, my neigh-bour, come a - way, See the work for us to-day, The hands to help, the mouths to feed, The sights to see, the books to read: Up and get us gone; to help the world a - long, Up and get us gone, my neigh - bour.

1 Up, my neighbour, come away,
See the work for us to-day,
The hands to help, the mouths to feed,
The sights to see, the books to read:

Up and get us gone, to help the world along,
Up and get us gone, my neighbour.

2 Up, my neighbour, see the plough
For our hands lies waiting now;
Grasp well the stilt, yoke up the team,
Stride out to meet the morning beam:

3 Up, my neighbour, see the land
Ready for the sower's hand;
The plough has made an even tilth,
The furrows wait the golden spilth:

4 Up, my neighbour, now the corn
Ripens at the harvest morn;
Then let it to our sickle yield,
And pile with sheaves the golden field:

5 Up, my neighbour, let us pray,
Thank our Maker every day,
Who gave us work our strength to test
And made us proud to do our best:

O Mo - ther dear, Je - ru - sa - lem, Je -ho - vah's throne on high,_____ O sa - cred ci - ty, queen, and wife Of Christ___ e - ter - nal - ly!_____

1   O Mother dear, Jerusalem,
        Jehovah's throne on high,
      O sacred city, queen, and wife
        Of Christ eternally!

2   O comely queen, in glory clad,
        In honour and degree;
      All fair thou art, exceeding bright,
        No spot there is in thee.

3   Thy part, thy shape, thy stately grace,
        Thy favour fair in deed,
      Thy pleasant hue and countenance,
        All others doth exceed.

4   O then thrice happy, should my state
        In happiness remain,
      If I might once thy glorious seat
        And princely place attain,

5   And view thy gallant gates, thy walls,
        Thy streets and dwellings wide,
      Thy noble troop of citizens
        And mighty King beside.

6   He is the King of kings, beset
        Amidst his servants' right;
      And they his happy household all
        Do serve him day and night.

7   O mother dear, Jerusalem,
        The comfort of us all,
      How sweet thou art and delicate;
        No thing shall thee befall!

Praise we the Lord, who made all beau - ty

For all our sen - ses to en - joy;

Owe we our hum - ble thanks and du - ty

That sim - ple plea - sures nev - er cloy;

Praise we the Lord who made all beau - ty

For all our sen - ses to en - joy.

1   Praise we the Lord, who made all beauty
        For all our senses to enjoy;
    Owe we our humble thanks and duty
        That simple pleasures never cloy;
    Praise we the Lord who made all beauty
        For all our senses to enjoy.

2   Praise him who makes our life a pleasure,
        Sending us things which glad our eyes;
    Thank him who gives us welcome leisure,
        That in our heart sweet thoughts may rise;
    Praise him who makes our life a pleasure,
        Sending us things which glad our eyes.

3   Praise him who loves to see young lovers,
        Fresh hearts that swell with youthful pride;
    Thank him who sends the sun above us,
        As bridegroom fit to meet his bride;
    Praise him who loves to see young lovers,
        Fresh hearts that swell with youthful pride.

4   Praise him who by a simple flower
        Lifts up our hearts to things above;
    Thank him who gives to each one power
        To find a friend to know and love;
    Praise him who by a simple flower
        Lifts up our hearts to things above.

5   Praise we the Lord who made all beauty
        For all our senses to enjoy;
    Give we our humble thanks and duty
        That simple pleasures never cloy;
    Praise we the Lord who made all beauty
        For all our senses to enjoy.

27

ROCKING
(Nativity)

Lit - tle Je - sus, sweet - ly___ sleep,
do not___ stir; We will___ lend a___
coat of___ fur, We will rock you,
rock you, rock you, We will rock you,

1 Little Jesus, sweetly sleep, do not stir;
  We will lend a coat of fur,
    We will rock you, rock you, rock you,
    We will rock you, rock you, rock you:
  See the fur to keep you warm,
  Snugly round your tiny form.

2 Mary's little baby, sleep, sweetly sleep,
  Sleep in comfort, slumber deep;
    We will rock you, rock you, rock you,
    We will rock you, rock you, rock you:
  We will serve you all we can,
  Darling, darling little man.

28

O LITTLE ONE

O Lit - tle One sweet, O Lit - tle One mild, Thy Fa - ther's pur - pose has been ful - filled; Thou cam'st from heaven to mor - tal ken, E - qual to be with us poor men, O Lit - tle One sweet, O Lit - tle One mild.

1 O little One sweet, O Little One mild,
Thy Father's purpose thou hast fulfilled;
  Thou cam'st from heaven to mortal ken,
  Equal to be with us poor men,
O Little One sweet, O Little One mild.

2 O Little One sweet, O Little One mild,
With joy thou hast the whole world filled;
  Thou camest here from heaven's domain,
  To bring men comfort in their pain,
O Little One sweet, O Little One mild.

3 O Little One sweet, O Little One mild,
In thee Love's beauties are all distilled;
  Then light in us thy love's bright flame,
  That we may give thee back the same,
O Little One sweet, O Little One mild.

JAMES HAWORTH & BROTHER, Ltd.
Music Engravers & Printers, London.

OXFORD UNIVERSITY PRESS